Praise for

Sell Like Crazy

This is about Ash Shukla's; his story of how he came to the United States from India with just $20 and not a word of English. Now, he has built a successful financial services business. For the first time ever, he pulls back the curtains as to how he built it. This Sell Like Crazy book is a must read book as he reveals his <u>5 Secret Steps To Building Your Empire</u> using CHAKRAS. I used just one of the 5 steps he teaches in an effort to win a contracting bid and was able to obtain a $50,000 bid in just 2 weeks. This Sell Like Crazy book by Ash Shukla gets CRAZY results!

----Eleni Marketis, President of Marketis Enterprises MBE & MDOT. Certified painting and contracting firm.

This book is the game changer that all business owners have been waiting for. This is a must read for all entrepreneurs, sales professionals, and anyone interested in getting unstuck in this sticky economy & increasing their sales revenue. The formula Ash lays out is simple, and easy to understand, and more importantly he lets us know that he is truly one of us. His sincerity truly bleeds through the pages as he explains his own rise from $20 in his pocket and not a word of English to building his multi-million dollar empire.

----- Trevor Otts Marketing Expert CEO of Broke Marketing Systems

Ash describes the importance of marketing in clear and concise terms, but also goes beyond the fundamentals by giving us a roadmap to follow. His book reminds us, in a subtle way, not to get so caught up in financial success that we forget the reason most of us strive so hard to succeed -- family.

----- Odessa Hopkins Owner of CEO Business Café

Sell Like Crazy

Evolution of an expert

5 Secret Steps To Building

Your Empire Using CHAKRAS

Be passionate, be intelligent and be the

Executor of ideas and your knowledge

By Ash Shukla

Sell Like Crazy

Evolution Of An Expert 5 Secret Steps To Building Your Empire Using CHAKRAS

By Ash Shukla

© 2012. This printing/edition 2015 Ash Shukla, All rights reserved.

ISBN-13: 978-0615732244 (Ash Shukla)

ISBN-10: 0615732240

Special Dedication

To My family whose motto is come together, stay together, and build together.

My family and me

Thank you for being my support & SBDC

(Small Business Development Center) for showing me the right path when I was looking for one.

Table Of Contents

Introduction

Debt is high and consumers are cash crunching. They used to spend $1.20 per dollar and now they are spending only $.80 on the dollar. What that means is that they are spending less on goods and services, and that is bad for business. Experts, Business Owners, and Entrepreneurs, who used to thrive, are taking a nosedive.

The questions are:

- Why are they taking a nosedive?

- What is the underlying reason?

Perhaps it could be that their chakras are off the mark.

Maybe they did not master the five steps of building their empire. Maybe they don't understand how chakras work in business and life. But most importantly, they don't understand how to use chakras and become the go-to expert, that way; they can earn more and work less.

The consumer used to be very open and fearless of spending money in the 90's. This is because the world was thriving, the debt was low, and they had money in the bank. This made the consumer feel powerful, energized, and unstoppable. Today the consumer is hanging on to their money. They are not spending. Instead, they are saving more than ever before because their gut feeling is full of scarcity and anxiety.

You see, in the past consumers made decisions based on their heart. They bought what they loved because they had excessive cash. Today the same consumer is making sure that every decision they make is the correct one for them. In other words, they are aligning their chakras before they make any buying decisions.

If they love what they see, instead of being impulsive, they wait and watch for it to go on sale. If it does go on sale, then they are asking, is this the right decision for me? And how would this affect my life later on down the road? They are thinking, working, and managing their *finances like a foreigner* who comes here with just $20 and doesn't speak a word of English.

Do you want to know why foreigners come to this country, go around the world and make it big? Well now you know.

I came here with $20 and didn't speak a word of English. My father took a risk of selling everything he owned and bought tickets to the land of opportunity.

On our way here we dreamed about driving a car, having a big house - where we all lived together, and having money in the bank. My parents gave me the blessings of my dreams. They blessed me with this gift of taking a ride with them to the land of opportunity. In 1989, we came here with a similar economy. However, while others saw problems of debt and taxes, we saw our cars, a big house, and money in the bank. And because of my parents' courage to give up everything for a single dream in making our future better, it gave me the courage to jump into business with nothing and build a successful business.

It helped to keep me going when I failed my insurance exam seven times, until I passed it the 8th time. It helped me when I went on appointment after appointment and didn't close any deals.

However, we kept on aligning our chakras, taking every step with careful consideration and making sure we were safe and secure, but yet moving forward. I have been fortunate to learn how to close 357% bigger transactions then the industry average and build a multi-million dollar empire, of which I am proud.

You too have the same opportunity as I had but the question is, are you going to focus on problems such as debt and taxes or the opportunity that lies ahead of you? Take a look at this: Despite the debt, the economy around the world is over Forty Trillion Dollars strong not counting the money that consumers have been saving by spending less. That means that if we just mesh in the economy, we have a Forty Trillion Dollars strong opportunity. If we tap into the consumer's bank account with world-class products and services - WOW what an opportunity we have to build your empire.

But perhaps you are thinking, why Ash, why are you doing this? Below are the five reasons I am writing this book:

1. To have a ticket with you so we can take a ride together, and build the empire of your dreams.

2. To help you understand what there are five fundamental steps that you must take to build your empire.

3. To help you understand how to align your personal, and business chakras with your target audience in order for you to build the legacy of your dreams.

4. To change the world's financial dynamics once and for all by building solid empires that not just survives, but thrives in any economy.

5. The most important reason is to make a difference in your friends and in your world. So, at the end of your life you get to say, "I loved every moment of my life, I lived every moment of my life, and YES! I did it." The score is settled.

I assume that you want to say just like I do, I lived and I loved every moment of my life, but best of all YES! I did it in my life. I was alive. You get to look down from the windows in the heaven and say, "Look, my children are safe and secure. My spouse is happy because I left them with a sense of security. The nonprofit I built is making a positive difference and it is now helping almost one million people. That consumer, who I helped, is enjoying my product and/or service. They are passing my product or service on to the next generation. WOW, what an empire I built! Look over there; I see no debt in the world. The world is living debt-free. I see that my best buddy, my friends, loved ones, his kids and my neighbors, they are wealthy and happy just because I passed this book on to them. They too have built an empire. The world has screen-less computers, and flying cars because of my innovation. Everyone around me is in a better place because of the risk I followed from my heart chakra, with implementing a roadmap, with the creative juice from my crown chakra, and took massive action from my gut chakra. My friends, family, and associates achieved all of that just because we went for it once and for all. "Our foreign friend Ash, who came here with just $20 and didn't speak a word of English - he encouraged me to take the plane ticket with him, and we did."

Chapter One

Let's take a plane ride together

It was September 4, 1989; we had waited nine years for this day to arrive. We were with 20 other family members, spending the last few moments at the Bombay International Airport. It was 7:00 P.M.; it was time for us to board the plane. Before we to walked towards the plane, we bowed to our elders, taking their blessings. As we walked towards the security gates, we knew that was the last time we would get to say "goodbye" for the next 20 years.

As we boarded the plane, we smelled the perfume and were taken by the fragrance. My parents, my brother and I walked into the plane for the very first time. We were completely blown away. I was in complete awe when I saw the maroon carpets, beige sidings, and the most fascinating part for me was the cabins and the knobs above my head. My brother and I were running down the aisle, fighting over the window seat. You see, I am the older brother; therefore, I had the distinct advantage! We decided to share the seat.

As we settled in the plane, I was seated next to the window, looking across from the runway at hundreds of people watching the plane. Among them was my family. As I waved goodbye to my family, I couldn't see that we pulled up on the runway. It was now 9:00 PM and time for us to take off.

We were sitting on the runway and the plane did not take off. It was now 10 P.M., 11 P.M., 12 A.M., 1 A.M. By that time, the pilot had announced there was a technical difficulty and the plane was hot and humid. It was very uncomfortable, to say the least.

How many times have you felt that your business or career was just not taking off due to technical difficulties?

How many times did you know you were about to take off but you just didn't know why you couldn't take the flight?

How many times have you felt like you were stuck on the runway?

Well, it's time that you took a flight, wouldn't you agree?

The plane finally took off at 1:30AM and we arrived at the London Heathrow Airport eight and a half hours later. As we entered the airport, we were in complete awe, eyeing the beauty around us. We could not believe how beautiful this airport was. "WOW" was the only word we could think about. I thought of a second word, BATHROOM. I had to go to the bathroom. We were at this beautiful airport, midway to our destination, at an unknown land, and we couldn't speak English. This was the most amazing thing we had ever seen. As we are trapping the beauty of this airport in our hearts, I had to go to the bathroom. I did not know how to ask, so I thought I could figure it out. As I was hunting for the bathroom I passed by a door that said "Restroom," which I thought was a V.I.P. room. Finally I found an Indian person who was able to point me in the right direction and I was able to finish my business.

As I walked up to my dad, I saw he was struggling at the counter. He was saying something the person at the ticket counter did not understand. And the ticket counter person was saying something we didn't understand, due to language barriers. This went on for about five minutes.

A nice Indian lady came up to us and helped us out. She helped translate what the ticket person was saying. What she said to us was not good. We had missed our connecting flight.

Have you ever had a feeling of being scared and confused in a situation that you don't understand how to get out of?

Have you ever been in a situation where you thought you were never going to make it to your destination?

We all felt that way and we thought we were doomed. We were scared and confused. We thought we were never going to make it to our destination. As we were panicking, the nice Indian lady told us that they were going to be giving us a ticket for the next morning flight and they were going to give us vouchers to stay overnight at a hotel, including food. We felt relieved as we accepted the tickets, and the food vouchers. After thanking that Indian lady, we went to the hotel. We were even excited to see the hotel for the first time. As we settled down in our room, we realized that we were all were very hungry. We went downstairs to the restaurant. We had two more problems, first we didn't understand what was on the menu, and second, we were vegetarians. Finding vegetarian food? Good luck. To our surprise the same lady walked up to us and helped us select items from the menu.

Little that we knew, we had picked a salad, spaghetti, and a roll. We had never seen these items before. You see my mom-cooked chapatti, parathas, curry, and vegetables at home every day. The concept of salad, spaghetti, and roll was totally new to us. But I thought, what the heck, I am hungry. Why not try this green grass first ("the salad"). It was just as I expected, horrible. Then I tried the spaghetti and that was horrible as well. At last I thought the bread couldn't be bad so I tried the bread and it turned out to be a soup roll and I could not bite the bread. Needless to say we went to bed hungry.

We could not sleep that night mainly because we were afraid that we were going to miss our connecting flight. Surely enough, the next morning, we got to the airport earlier then we had planned-just to be certain that we did not miss the flight again.

As we took off my dad and I were having an intimate conversation and we talked about how we would be driving a car, owning a big house, where we lived together, and having money in the bank to secure our future. I said, "Dad, thanks for taking this risk," as I promised myself that no matter what - that dream will come true.

Another nine hours later, the plane had arrived at JFK and a few hours later we arrived at our final destination, Washington Dulles International Airport.

First thing I did, I exclaimed, "I have arrived!" I kissed the ground, did my little dance, and promised to do something great.

When you arrive at your destination how will you celebrate your victory?

_____

_____

_____

_____

_____

_____

How many times have you felt that your business will never take off the ground due to technical difficulties in your business chakras?

_____

_____

How many times have you felt your business chakras are not aligning and you feel stuck? You feel as though your plane has landed at the Heathrow Airport, and now you are not going to make it to your destination because you don't know who to ask, or who to turn to for help. You don't even know what to do and how to move forward because the new world you have entered has a whole new language.

_____

_____

_____

_____

_____

At a time like this, you need someone who will not just give you the ticket and remind you of your intimate inner promise you made to your dreams and tell you that everything is going to be just fine, but get on the plane ride with you. I am here to take the ride all the way to your destination. I am here to help you chart the way to your dreams. You can feel free to contact me at Ash@ FinancialChakras.com or Call: 410-493-3358 any time.

While we take this wonderful journey together let me ask you a question. If you could have a business that ran without you and you could live the life of your dreams, what would that life be like? If you could say at the end "Yesssss I did it," what would that be?

_____

_____

_____

_____

_____

_____

_____

_____

Let me give you a hint as to how you can accomplish your dream. Understand and implement three chakras.

Let's take the ride as I explain to you what chakras are and how they can help you reach your dream of having a business that runs without you, as it did for me.

NOTES

Are you ready to take the plane ride together?

_____

I would like to learn the following during this

Plane ride....

_____
_____
_____
_____
_____
_____
_____
_____
_____
_____
_____
_____
_____
_____
_____
_____
_____
_____
_____

Chapter Two

The Chakras

When I speak to people, they always ask me:

- What are chakras and how do they affect us?

- How can chakras help me personally and professionally?

- Where do chakras originate?

- What does the word Chakra mean?

In this chapter, I am going to explain all of this to you in a brief synopsis. I am not going to make you a chakra expert, better yet; I am going to help you gain a better understanding of chakras so you can see how you can use them in your personal and professional life.

I am so eager to teach this to you because I have used chakras in my personal life and professional life. I struggled in business for seven years until I discovered my grove of chakras

Let me share some results of how using chakras in my business helped me:

- My business went from struggling to over $2 million.

- I have closed 357% higher transactions than my industry average.

- I have created world-class marketing and branding.

- I have written books, made CDs, DVDs, online programs, built speeches, and designed seminars and presentations that made people go, "Wow, that was the best of the best!"

My clients have understood and used chakras. They achieved amazing results. So why not you?

What are chakras and where do they come from?

There are seven points or Chakras in our bodies that shape us, physically, emotionally, and spiritually.

The three emotional triggers are:

1.   Love,

2.   Intellect/Intelligence,

3.   Intuition/Certainty.

When these chakras align correctly, the decisions we make turn out to be correct ones. But whenever we end up making a wrong decision, it is certain that one of them was off the mark. The irony is that these chakras are not just part of human bodies but they are the law of the universe.

Where did chakras come from?

Chakras came from India, where yogis did yoga, and used Ayurveda *medication* to heal. Ayur means life and Veda means medication - Life medication. This came about in 2500B.C. When yogis did yoga, they did it to align their chakras. They wanted to ensure that they did not get sick and had a healthy and prosperous life. Their mission was to give back to the world. Because the Crown chakra, this chakra sits on top of your head, which is your connection of divine giving. This is the reason you were born. This is the reason you were put on earth.

So, give and you shall receive. Does this sound familiar? You need to take your gift of understanding others' needs and give to the world. As an author, speaker, seminar leader, online marketer, coach, information marketer and business owner, you are here to leave a legacy. So align your chakras and give back because the world is waiting to hear from you.

What happens when chakras are not aligned?

Chakras not inline:

- Have you ever made a decision where you were wrong? Think of a time in your life when you made a decision, which you regret even today.

- Have you ever bought something from a store and then you returned it?

- Did you ever make a decision where you asked, "Why did I do that?

Chakras Inline:

- Have you ever seen a marketing piece where you were in complete awe?

- Have you ever purchased something where you felt the person or entity just understood you and were in fact helping you?

- Did you think to yourself that that was an amazing experience and I would go to buy more of whatever they have to sell over and over again?

- Did you ever think, "How did they know that?"

To put it simply, they understand what chakras do to attract at every given time so that you would end up with their products and services, no matter what the price.

This happened to me when I met the woman of my dreams. My wife used chakras to attract me. During our meeting I asked a question, "What do you like to do?" Let me disclose something here. I thought my wife was pretty right from the get go. So, yes, you can say I have and had the hots for her from the moment I saw her. She replied, "Well I am a classical Indian dancer." She has done a masters course in that. I thought hummm... she is a traditional Indian. Love it! Then she said, "I have a master's degree in business administration." I thought dang, she is smart too! My God! I thought you are singing my song and you have hit me in the gut. Of course, I proposed to her immediately and we said, "YES" to each other in just three minutes and got married the next month.

Oh, by the way, did this happen to you when you met your woman or man.

Ladies just know how to use Chakras better then men in every aspect of life, that's it.

By using these Chakras and aligning them correctly will help you eliminate mistakes and increase your chances for success. Look at these guys who do multi-million dollars in business:

Warren Buffet

He lost money in a deal in his early years of investing. At that time he lost about eight or nine thousand dollars. To him it was a big deal. What he discovered was that he would not have made that deal had he known what he was getting into. What he did was some soul searching and he decided that he is going to do the investing, which is his passion. However, he was going to do three things. In my studies of Warren Buffett, I have discovered this:

1. He always made sure that he falls in love with whatever the investment he is going to make, hence he makes sure that his Heart Chakra is in line.

2. He then studies the stock or investment he is going to make thoroughly in utmost detail, hence satisfying the Intelligence chakras.

3. Then he waits for that investment or stock to go on sale before he goes for the kill and finally the moment of buying comes where he buys the investment or stock, hence exercising the gut chakra.

Note: He never makes a decision unless he is certain all three chakras have aligned.

Steve Jobs

Let's settle on one thing that Steve Jobs loved -Apple. He did not like it; he ate, breathed, and slept thinking about Apple. His heart chakra was there.

In developing products he used his passion for Apple to help him thrive. His genius was the creation of Apple in a way that lives in the 25th century. While others thought about this century, he thought about the future and built products accordingly. When you own Apple products, you know that it has intelligence written all over it. This is his Head Chakra; this is the chakra of intelligence.

Now let's look at Steve's gut chakra. When he developed a product he looked at ease of use, high class, and product differentiation to the consumer.

If you read the books that are about him you will see that it is written all over that Steve's Heart Chakra, Head Chakra, and the Gut Chakra were in what he did all the time, every time. When they were not aligning, he drove his engineers crazy. He pushed them to the end. That is why he made history. That is why he was one of the great ones.

Whether you look at Warren Buffett, Steve Jobs, or any other genius you will see that all of these chakras are present.

This is the reason why I wanted to talk to you about chakras - not only that, but I want to help you create products and programs. And to help you evolve as an expert- The Go To Expert and serve that higher purpose that you are here to fulfill.

I want to teach you chakras so you can rise above others and become a recognized expert in the world.

In the coming chapters, I am going to teach you how to use chakras to become the expert in sales, marketing, niche, and dream creation.

I am including a piece of chakras in this book, but in the next book, "The 7 Chakras of Business," I am going to teach you how chakras work in your business so you can have the business of your dreams.

For now, though, let me show you what happened to me and how I used chakras so you can see how you can use them in your life and business.

NOTES

What questions would you like me to answer about chakras when you meet me live at my event?

_____

_____

_____

_____

_____

_____

_____

_____

_____

What can I help you solve using chakras?

_____

_____

_____

_____

_____

_____

_____

_____

_____

_____

What is one thing that you learned about chakras that were surprising to you?

_____

_____

_____

_____

_____

_____

_____

How would you use chakras in your life if you knew how much they could help you?

_____

_____

_____

_____

_____

_____

_____

_____

_____

_____

_____

_____

_____

_____

_____

Chapter Three

Persistence pays dividends

Have you ever thought about living a legacy and making your dreams a reality?

Have you ever sat down and wondered how you can achieve the dream you always wanted to go after?

If I know and understand you - I know you have wondered about that. You have thought about making your dreams a reality, haven't you? You even tried to achieve it time and time again. In the effort to achieving your dreams, you sacrificed your time, effort, and the last bit of savings you had, haven't you? You went after it with the glimpse of hope and gave it all you had, and most of the time it turned into disappointment.

To your surprise it worked when you tried it in the 1990's. It worked so well that you became unstoppable. You became the force to be reckoned with. You felt like an eagle flying high in the sky. You felt like you were untouchable. You did not know, nor did you care about why it worked. All you knew was that it worked and you were happy counting the CASH in the bank.

Little did you know, the economy gave up on you and now you are wondering, where are those "good old days?" What happened to that dream life I had imagined? At that moment you felt stuck at the London Heathrow Airport like we did. You can't speak or communicate the language of the new economy. You don't know

31

who to ask, how to ask, and where to turn for the answers to your questions. You don't know what to do next so that you can get back up and fly again, just like the Bald Eagle. You are wondering what I am going to do next to make everything work again. You are strategizing, and working long hours but it is just not working. Some people are in the brinks of giving up and throwing in the towel.

That is why I am here to tell you my story. Not a boasting story, but a story of failure, lessons I learned, and how I pulled out of a situation that defies many odds.

My Story

I had nothing but just $20 in my pocket, and didn't speak a word of English; I had the heart of a lion in a tiny bird's body. Let this bird tell you its story so that you can fly too.

It was 1994. I was going to college studying computer science, and minor in math. During my college years I was looking for odds and ends of jobs to pay for college. I ran into the financial services field. I had gotten an opportunity to work with subsidiary of City Corp, as an independent contractor. Little that I knew, on the second day of my work I ended up going to a convention that changed my life.

This convention was held at The Georgia Dome in Atlanta. Upon arrival at the dome, I saw 60,000 people running around excited about their life. They were all there with a mission of achieving their dreams. They were there determined to conquer and overcome the odds.

In the morning of the first day of the event, I sat down in the doghouse seat at the top left of the dome. As I sat and observed that there were all these people excited and cheering for their dreams -as though it had already come true, I thought - WOW! I felt the passion they had along with their excitement.

Soon the leaders started speaking. They started to talk about how excited they were there to see all of us. They were delivering messages filled with hope and excitement. They were telling the crowd about what they had learned in life and business. During the opening ceremony, a speaker mentioned that you should commit to your craft, invest in yourself, and never give up, In spite of all the encouraging words, all I could think about was the excitement in the room and how I could stand at the podium to see what it was like to view 60,000 people. During the brake I figured out a way and snuck up to the podium. I stood at the podium for a few minutes as my manager said, "pssss, Ash, pssss, get off the podium." Ignoring his whispering, I was just taking that scene and installing it in my heart. I was capturing the moment, and enjoying looking left and right. I have to tell you that was the best moment. What a moment that was!

Throughout the event I met many leaders and gained lots of wisdom. At the age of 21, gaining that knowledge was so important to me. The end of the convention was even more exciting. There were fireworks, balloons, and confetti. I caught one and wrote down my dream that my dad and I discussed. The dream that I promised myself, is that I would make it provide for my family in having a car, a big house, and having money in the bank.

From 1989 to 1994 my parents, my brother, and I had achieved more than most could have imagined. But now this was my turn. It was my turn to make it happen. I felt I had found a perfect opportunity to make my mark, live my legacy, and make my dreams come true.

I came home all excited and went for my insurance exam for the very first time. I had to get a minimum score of 70. I failed it the first time. I received 69 points. I thought ok, no problem, let's do it again. A couple of weeks later I went and I failed it again, I received 68. I went for the Third time, and I received 67. The fourth time 66, fifth time 67, sixth time 68. By now I had heard about the OJ Simpson trial and learned the word prejudice and thought the computer was prejudice. I called the computer prejudice. I also thought that guy who checked me in for the exam, was pushing buttons on the screen and changing my answers. Hmm... something is fishy, I thought.

I decided to change the testing center and went to DC. But this time I was not just mad I was angry. I really had to pass the test to even get paid. So this time I took the book and used my visualization memory and memorized the book word for word, inside and out. The second thing I did was to change the testing center from Bowie State University to the Washington DC testing center. Well needless to say I received 69 points. I was disappointed and depressed. It was so bad; I did not know how to break the news to my parents.

Have you ever been in a situation where you were disappointed, but you were so close to achieving your goals you could feel it in your bones?

I felt the same way, so I picked myself back up again and read that book one more time. But this time I had been looking for a last piece of information, which could help me, pass the test. I figured from the state's life and health insurance department that they gave students with English as a second language, one hour extra time to comprehend the material during the test. That, was the key that unlocked the doors and I passed the exam.

I went for my investment exam and passed that as well and finally became a financial advisor.

Lessons I learned:

- Be persistent

- Never give up

- Put in 150% effort not just 70%

Now it was time for me to finally earn some money. I set appointments by calling my friends, family members, and everyone I knew and set 5-20 appointments per week. I would go on appointment after appointment but could not close any deals. After running out of a warm market, I even tried cold calling and every method you can imagine possible to get more appointments. I tried and tried for seven years to make my dream of having a business a reality. I tried again and again setting appointments having no shows and disappointments from these appointments day in and day out.

There were days I thought am I ever going to make it and go beyond pain and agony. There were days I had self-doubts to say the least. By now I saw that my friends were settling down and I felt as though I was being left behind. I found myself again in the same situation.

What kept me going were self-improvement books, audiotapes, videotapes, seminars and boot camps. I even hired personal coaches to help me. Since then, it is normal for me to spend $500 per month in self-improvement. Self-improvement kept me sane. It kept me going when I came from a hard day at work and did not make any money. That kept me going when I went on my fifth appointment and did not close that deal. Self-improvement kept my "fire burning."

My question to you is, "how much money do you invest in self-improvement on a regular basis?" My guess is not enough. My advice to you is go ahead and keep doing it. Here is a way I looked at it. College costs $40,000 per year. Multiply that by four and you would have spent $160,000 just for the tuition.

And what do you get for it, a job and a paycheck that keeps you safe and secure. Friends, this is the future that you are looking forward too. But what I wanted was beyond this. I wanted something spectacular. I wanted to be and do something that is unimaginable. I wanted to ring the gong and tell the world, "HEY WORLD I AM HERE." That is what has kept me going at all times.

Here is what happened after seven years of pain and agony.

I got a job at a bank as a branch manager. I surpassed the goals of the Bank, twice! My branch received the honor of winning a huge competition. Then I became an investment banker across from the treasury building for another major bank. If that is not enough, I decided to go into business for myself in the financial services industry. But this time it was different. This time I felt in my bones that I could go beyond, because of the knowledge and experience I had gained. This time I was not going to take any chances. I was going to make sure that my chakras were aligned.

Chakra #1 Love

Chakra #2 Intelligence

Chakra #3 Intuition

Chakra #1 - Love: I knew I loved what I did. That was a given.

Chakra #2 - Intelligence: I had a dream and I thought every step through from whom I was going to go after as a target audience. How I was going to attract them so they would come to me instead of me going after them? How I was going to do business with them and gain more referrals from them so I could continue the business? And the last step was what propelled my business, which was to become the "go-to expert" in my field.

Chakra #3 - Execution: I executed a plan of action that took my business from struggling to multi-million dollar in five short years.

Here are the results:

- I made $800,000 in just three mouths of being in business. I made $1,200,000 the second year, $1,400,000 third year, $1,600,000 fourth year, $2,000,000 plus the fifth year.

- I invested $500 per month for 18 years = $108,000 and I build my dream empire. I built a business that can run without me, a business that went from struggling to multi-million dollars in just five short years after the struggle.

During these seven years, I had learned some valuable lessons:

Lesson #1 - No matter what, don't quit

Lesson #2 - Work hard everyday

Lesson #3 - Learn from your mistakes

Lesson #4 - Invest in yourself monthly

Lesson #5 - Get smart and find your own groove

At the end I achieved my dream of having a car, house, and money in the bank.

But above all, as a business owner and as a foreigner, I built a business that ran without me. An achievement I am proud of.

If you lay the groundwork and align the chakras of your business you too can go beyond your dreams. You too can achieve anything you want. You too can start with just $20 and build an empire you are proud of. Let me show you how in the next few chapters.

Are <u>YOU</u> ready?

My question to you is, "Are you willing to make the commitment it takes to build an empire you are proud of?

Are you willing to stop playing dead and come to life just once and light the fire inside you?

If you are ready to take a flight again and be the eagle say, "YES! I am READY!"

Say it, "I am READY!"

I know you may be reading this in public but just do the gesture and say, "YES!" I am READY! Or if you want yell it out, "YES! I am READY!"

Ok, I will see you in the next chapter when we talk about picking your target audience.

NOTES

What is the main reason you want to build your empire?

_____
_____
_____
_____
_____
_____

What are three tangible benefits you will receive by perusing your dream?

_____
_____
_____
_____
_____
_____
_____
_____

What is that one dream that you keep seeing over and over again?

_____
_____
_____
_____

Every time you want to give up you will do following ritual.

_____

_____

_____

I would invest following per month in myself to get better at what I do.

Circle one.

1. $300

2. $500

3. $750

4. $2,000

Mistakes I keep making which I need to change are....

_____

_____

_____

_____

_____

_____

_____

_____

_____

Additional NOTES

Chapter Four

Choose to go after a target audience

Have you ever wondered if you should go after a target audience?

If you go after a target audience, would your business really be that much better?

The answer is YES!

I can tell you from experience that if you go after a specific niche, your business will be that much better. You will actually begin to have a life and a business.

Finding my Groove

Let me share with you what I used to do when I could not find my groove. In the beginning of my career in 1994, I wasn't making much money. I could not find my groove. There were for several reasons for this, however, one of them was not having a target audience. My boss constantly told me go get more business, but never told me who to go after. So naturally I thought the whole world was my target audience. Every day I would wake up and wonder what is it that I am supposed to do today? Who will me to call today? What am I going to say to these people? Where would I meet these people? This was a constant battle for me. After about half a day of wondering, I would make calls and set up some appointments. Because I did not know much about my audience; I did not know what to say or where to begin, much less closing the deal. I would give the presentation, which was taught like a robot and consequently, I made no money. That meant I could not ask for referrals. I could not answer their concerns or questions. It was a new experience every time and there was no predictability. This cost me thousands of hours and seven years of my life, time with my family, and doing the things I enjoyed.

You see, <u>not knowing</u> was perhaps the most costly mistake I made. In my estimates I spent over 12,000 hours of my life just listening to self-improvement and spent over $110,000 just understanding how to build my empire. That is why I tell business owners that you have a choice to spend that much time and money. Or... you could just come to the **"LIVE"** - Sell Like Crazy Academy and we will teach you what to do and avoid what not to do, in order to accelerate your business and success.

I don't want you to fall into the same trap that I did. That is why I am telling you that you too need to focus on picking a niche.

Here is how to pick a niche:

In 2004, after purchasing my dream home, I decided to go in business for myself. After establishing the name of my Firm, I decided to get some assistance. During this conversation, I learned that I needed to select a niche. Thank God I listened! Based on previous knowledge and Theorell research I decided to pick a specific niche. This changed the game forever.

Listening to this wise man's advice, I chose to go after Baby Boomers and Retirees. I decided to go after this market for several reasons:

First, I love to work with this audience.

Second, I knew the history of this audience.

I knew for a fact that this is the group of people that took Gerber baby food from 50,000 jars to 5 million jars in sales. As this group got older, they played with toys and the toy industry boomed. As they got into the teen stage the fast food industry boomed. McDonald's, Pizza Hut, etc. started to accelerate. As this group got older, got married, and had children, even the real estate industry boomed. And now this wave is about to hit age 65 and I didn't want to miss the wave that is going to hit the retirement planning industry.

Third, I knew this audience inside and out.

I knew their four keys of making the decisions. Their likes, dislikes, wants, and needs.

This is what gave me the foresight I needed to attract, acquire, cultivate, motivate, and position myself before the competition. This kept me ahead of the competition all the time.

Most people would have stopped there and that would have been fine, but what I did is that I actually choose a niche as an audience, a marketing strategy, and products that specifically serves my prospect well beyond their needs. So I actually was ultra-niche. I followed this to a tee. This gave me the edge. It took me three months of research before I decided to do my first marketing campaign.

For my audience, I choose the Boomers and Retirees. I choose safety-oriented measures to preserve their retirement venues. This is where we preserved 100% of what they had and moved on from there. I was so confident that I gave my audience 100% assurance that this is going to work out by giving them a specific laddered approach. In this approach we addressed the two biggest concerns they had. One: concern about running out of money. Second: losing their principle and gains in the bad markets. In my solutions we inserted safety measures that were 100% insured and guaranteed so that my clients can sleep peacefully by knowing that they will not run out of money at old age, and never lose their principle and gains.

This is one of the reasons my business went from a start up to $800,000 in 3 months. That is the reason when markets shifted I did not lose a dime for my clients and won their hearts and minds. It is also the reason my clients never leave me because I took care of them well beyond their needs. This is precisely why I have been able to build perpetual marketing where business never stops.

Having a niche plays a major role in your business. When you don't pick a niche it will cost you thousands of hours and hundreds of thousands of dollars. In my attempt to figure this out I was listening to self-improvement tapes, reading books, and going to seminars, I have invested over 12,000 hours and over $108,000 just to understand the lessons I am teaching you.

The best thing I can tell you is pick the niche. It will save you tons of time, effort and sleepless nights. It will give you the freedom and the structure you need to build a business that can run without you.

So what is the formula to pick your niche, you ask?

First understand that there are two types of niches you can pick:

Niche One: You go after specific markets or groups

1. Pick the audience that you love to work with.

2. Determine if this audience makes logical sense financially, physically, and emotionally.

3. Determine an execution strategy that will be the most effective in the current market condition.

Niche Two: Your product is the niche.

1. Build a product that would capture your audience emotionally.

2. Build your product so that it would make logical sense.

3. Build your product so that it is easy to use and in a class by itself.

Now, all you have to do is pick your niche. So my question to you is this, of the two types of niches, which one suits you the best? All I have to say is pick your niche and be rich.

You may be scared and wondering that if you pick a niche you would earn less and can't attract everyone.

What I have discovered is that if you pick a niche the following things happen:

- Develop a clear marketing direction

- Spend less money on marketing

- Understand your clients better

- Meet specific needs of your clients, hence developing clients and not customers

- Gain referrals since this is the best way to increase business

- Charge more for your service

- Become well known and brand faster and cheaper

In a nutshell, picking a niche helps you earn more and work less. So go ahead and pick your niche and you, my friend, deserve to be rich.

NOTES

What target audience would you like to go after?

Hint Pick 3 – 5 Examples

_____

_____

_____

_____

_____

_____

_____

Which audience makes logical sense financially, physically, and emotionally?

_____

_____

_____

_____

_____

_____

What execution strategy will be most effective in targeting this audience?

_____

_____

_____

_____

Chapter Five

"The Marketing Maze"

How do you view marketing? This is a question that I frequently ask people. Every single time the answer I get from business owners and entrepreneurs, who are the Eagles of the economy, is that they are confused. They tell me it is a maze that they can't figure out.

This maze is so confusing that it has two components:

1. You have off-line marketing, which has to do with the **human factor**.

2. There is the online factor, which has to do with the **Internet.**

If that is not enough, both of these components have a microcosmic set of actions to reach a particular audience. This microseism of activity has made the world of marketing even more confusing and mysterious. I used to feel the same way. Don't worry; we will solve this mystery of off-line and online marketing in this chapter.

Many business owners, Entrepreneurs, Authors, Speakers, Seminar leaders, Internet marketers, and coaches believe that marketing is a maze and often get confused on how to solve this maze. I totally understand the fact that marketing could be and is also a very complex subject in today's economy. In addition, marketing is a maze because we, as creators, focus on doing everything at once instead of getting great at one campaign, and mastering one medium at a time. The fact is your business requires one to three mediums of marketing along with my three secret steps to build world-class campaigns, which I will cover in this book.

To help you frame your thinking, allow me to offer you some direction. First, stop thinking complex and think simple. Second, don't think hard, think easy. Third, you need to stop thinking how and start thinking what. For example, what's the next step? Fourth, you need to think offline and online as two different ways to market. Fifth, stop thinking, oh my God, what the heck am I going to do now, instead, think wow look what I can do. You need to stop thinking local and think global.

Develop the thinking of a treasure hunt. Every time you do a campaign it should be a treasure hunt. It's a hunt for more names, e-mail addresses, and social media likes and then it becomes the hunt for new clients and not customers.

In 1994 the only thing I knew about marketing was that I needed to call the people I knew and had relationships with. When I ran out of my market the only other thing I knew was that I had to somehow meet people. Since I did not have the target audience picked out, I thought everyone was my client. When someone told me you need to do prospecting, I got excited and kept on going out and meeting people. However, I kept on running into a wall of disappointments. As time went on, this became more difficult. It became a near impossible task. It got to be very frustrating. I felt like that dog chasing his tail. The only thing I had going for me was the hope of making my dream and promise to myself come true.

Unfortunately, the hope of making your dreams come true is not enough to make your dreams a reality. This rude awakening and self-realization was the core of my success from 2004 onwards.

Perhaps you are at a point where you are also feeling this rude awakening. You realize that without having a strategy this is not going to work. Without having an execution plan this is simply not going to happen. So I hope you are sitting down for this one. This is going to take some time for us to discuss. During this time of trial and error what I learned is that there are three main chakras to offline and online marketing.

The Chakras of Marketing

- Marketing must appeal to your prospects immediately. Your marketing needs to make them go "WOW!"

- Marketing needs to be targeted and focused.

- Marketing must engage them intellectually. Your marketing needs to fill the need that they have been experiencing.

- Marketing must engage your prospects through a process that will lead them to your desired outcome with the least amount of investment from your pocket. This is the ultimate marketing goal.

- Marketing needs to be out of the box, ahead of its time, and not the same old stuff.

- Marketing must fit your personality.

- Marketing needs to be cost-effective which brings high profits.

Based on this formula I started my business in 2004. Knowing this formula helped me plan and prepare better.

So, this time it is going to be different and I knew it. I remembered my experience before and I was going to make sure that I didn't repeat the same mistakes again. That would be stupid, wouldn't you agree? So this time I chose the Boomers and Retirees market place, and I chose to serve the market in a particular way. I chose to serve the market with my strength of doing seminars and training. I chose to spend the money to attract clients and follow the non-traditional route of marketing.

I chose to do seminar marketing for several reasons:

1. It was a way to mail to the audience of our choice. This is what we call precise marketing where I chose the age, gender, assets, income, and geography.

2. This was the new way to market. This was so effective that when I did a mailing, 200 people showed up at my first event.

3. This was ahead of the curve, and at this point not many financial advisors were doing this.

4. This gave the prospects the opportunity to get to know who I am and how I can help.

5. This gave me a chance to weed out non-interested prospects from interested ones in just two hours vs. the alternative.

6. This gave me a chance to build the level of trust like nothing before.

7. The most important reason I chose to do this was because public speaking is my strength. I know if I get in front of a group of people, I can make it happen.

To sum this up, here is what happened from this marketing activity:

Wedding style invitations: 5,000 pieces @ .83 cents

Response rates: 2-5%

Plate lickers: 10%

Ideal audience: 90%

Mailing cost: approximately $4,000

Food cost: $4,000

Total cost of doing business: $8,000

Revenue per event: $70,000

Profit: $62,000

Now that you have chosen your target market, let me ask you a question about marketing. What one thing can you implement right away that lets you operate from your strength and it is ahead of your competition?

Different times require different marketing techniques.

In 2008 I saw that now more than ever many boomers are hitting the age of 65. These people are retiring in waves and all the financial professionals, banks, and brokers are in the game of doing seminar marketing. This poses a couple of problems. One, we have to mail 6,000 pieces of mail vs. 5,000 due to the drop in response rates. Second, there were more people sitting in the seminar just for the food. Third, the costs of food and stamps had gone up. Forth, there were less people showing up at these events due to heavy competition.

Wedding style invitations: 6,000 @ $1.25

Response rates: 1-3%

Plate lickers: 25-40%

Ideal audience: 75-60%

Food cost: $6,000

Total cost of doing business: $13,500

Revenue per event: $70,000

Profit: $56,500

Now you may be looking at this and going this is not bad and I agree it is not bad at all. But I wondered what if there is a better way to market. What if there is a way that would reduce the cost but yet keep the money in my bank account. I thought of a couple of new strategies and the strategy was this: I took a small trash can; about 4 inches tall and 3 inches in diameter and put a letter in the trash can stating that I am a financial professional and I know that you were going to trash this letter so I did it for you. This was a hit.

Mailing size: 100-peace @ 2.50

5-10% responses

5 appointments

3 closes

Average revenue per close: $20,000

Total Revenue: $60,000

Profit: $59,500

Risk only: $250

Benefit: No competition

But to top this off, what I am about to tell you next are my secret weapons, so listen up. Whether I spent $10,000 on marketing or $250 in marketing; during this entire process what I implemented was the idea of "**NEXT**." Before, I sat down with a couple and discussed our agreement. I called it the karma agreement. This agreement basically stated that I am **NOT** going to charge you any fee for my visits and my time. But in return, you agree that you would provide me with three warm introductions.

My Secret Weapons

1. **What is a warm introduction?**

Name, e-mail, and phone number where you have formally introduced me as someone you trust as an advisor.

At the kitchen table we would sit down and make a list of the people they know. Then I would have the prospects send letters out to at least the top three people they knew. During this time I would call the people from the list and start setting appointments.

This is a game changer for me.

Marketing cost: $1.26

Revenue: $20,000

Woo Hooooo!

2.   Birthday Parties

My next secret weapon is my birthday parties. You know husbands normally forget their wife's birthday or anniversary. So I put together a surprise lunch or dinner for the wife. The husband was asked to invite three to five close friends and family members to join us in the celebration of his wife's birthday. They all would come and sit down at this big table and wish her a happy birthday. Of course here I come walking in without saying anything and I sit down in a chair, which has been placed next to the wife and husband. At this point everyone wonders who is this guy? The wife immediately says this is Ash our financial advisor and he did a wonderful job for us, and we haven't seen him in a week. Of course everyone laughs and we have an icebreaker. From this activity I would gain about 90% of them as clients.

This is how it went:

Marketing cost: $250

Revenue: $60,000+

As you can see, I constantly think of new ways to invent to reduce the cost of marketing and increase profits.

3.   Financial Game

My latest invention is a financial game that teaches my audience members how the financial markets work. This game is made from the most beloved games in the US history. It's a fun game. You should join us.

This is where my audience pays me to come and play the game. My cost of marketing has gone to zero and perhaps even in positive territory, due to sponsorship opportunities for other business owners.

By the way, if you have a group that would like to play this game full of education, just send me an e-mail at: Ash@FinancialChakras. com and I would love to play it with you and your group.

Here are the results:

E-Mail marketing: 5,000 E-mails

My cost: $0

Response: 1-5%

Attendee's pay: $30 to join and eat lunch.

My cost for lunch: $0

Sponsors: $500 each @ 2 - 4 sponsors

Profit per event: $70,000

With this I would like to invite you to play this game. With this game you will be able to learn the cool concept of how the market works in real time. Why losing money in the market does not make any sense?

Marketing doesn't have to be expensive, but it has to be clever. It has to make your audience come to you. The best way to market is to have zero expenses and maximize profits.

Of the strategies discussed, which strategy makes most sense to you?

What strategies can you come up with that would help you take your marketing from ordinary to extra ordinary?

BZZZT Marketing

- How can I implement an effective strategy?

- What strategy fits modern times?

- Well, well, well wouldn't you like to know?

So you ask how can I do that?

I was going to tell you that anyway. To do this, let me take you back so you can see the future.

I call this the BZZZZZ marketing. Let's go in the past so I can show you the future.

Imagine its 1775 and you are off on an island and your goal is to find the hidden treasure on the island. The trick is that you have to reach as many people as you can on this island with a compelling message. This message is so awesome that it has to be delivered. Your products and services are so great they have to be sold. So not knowing any better, you think immediately, what are the possible ways you can deliver this message? Oh wait, you think, I can use newspapers and mail because the first post office just opened. "WOW," I can place my advertisement in the newspapers and send out letters to everyone as a follow-up. You do this and people begin to congratulate you, you get famous but at a hefty price. Over time your competition is doing the same and now it's getting impossible to maintain the cost of doing business.

Now you passed away and your kids are running your business and passing that message along to the world. Its 1890's, Nikola Tesla just demonstrated that it's possible to transmit the energy over radio. So everyone is excited and now the news spreads like wild fire. Radio and telephones are the things of the future. The news is traveling faster and the legacy you left behind is spreading even faster than you thought. As you look from that window in heaven you are proud to see that business is booming because you left that legacy and your kids are doing great.

But now your kids have passed away as well and they are with you looking through that window from above and seeing how your grandkids are doing. Your grandkids have adopted the business and now its 1930's and the first television was created. Everyone is excited about this new gadget and everyone is buying one and it's becoming the most common and effective way to communicate your message. As a matter of fact, it's so powerful that it helps sell millions of copies of your book, which contains your message.

Your grandkids pass away as well so now it's the 1950's and you and your kids decide to come back so you take the elevator back down to earth to continue your family legacy because you want to spread your message even further. Until the early 2000's mail, newspaper, radio, and television worked great. However, you are searching for a better solution then mail, newspaper, radio, and television because they are getting more expensive than ever before. You can't sustain this. What you don't realize is that industrial age is gone. It doesn't exist. Now we are in the information age. Out of frustration you and your kids go on a vacation where you are relaxing near the beach. Then you noticed that there are people who are touching this cable, which has this magical power, and every time they touch it the cable zaps them. The cable has this magical power and it actually makes them more powerful. At first you think NO WAY! NO! NO! This can't be real so you ignore it. But you noticed everyone on the island is doing this. Your kids grab this cable and it makes them unstoppable.

You decide to check this cable out a little closer. But you are not sure. When you look at it like, you think what the heck is this? In this waiting game, time passes by you. It's now 2012 and your kids have been asking dad, "What the heck is wrong with you?" Touch the cable and see the power of this ionic cloud called the Internet. You ask whaaaaaat? The Internet? What is that? Your children explain to you that it is a transport device, which transfers information faster, cheaper, and more efficiently than ever before. It helps you connect to the people on other islands and this water sends messages and they are delivered through electricity. Your children ask you, - "Dad, just take the cable." Low and behold you are zapped. You feel a tingling sensation in your body. You begin to feel an unknown power. You know deep down inside you that this is big. As soon as you touch it you see this cloud appear and in the cloud comes the video for WWW. This is the birth of the Internet. It teaches you how you can communicate to the world and spread your message with a touch of a finger; in addition, you will be spending little to no money. But wait that's not all. You'll see that social media comes along to help you connect even faster with their communities. The combination of E-Mails and Social media are so powerful that you feel like you have the world in your hands. You are spending pennies and earning dollars - you finally feel more powerful. This all happened just because you got zapped. Now you can earn more and work less. You know you can finally sustain that business, but better yet you can deliver your message via social networks and e-mails. You're the man!

But wait, you say wait a minute. What am I supposed to do with all of this stuff? Now I know how to do offline and online marketing.

I have a website, E-Mail, Facebook, Twitter, LinkedIn, YouTube, and other channels. They are all great but I don't know what to do and where to turn to understand them. How am I supposed to put this in an order so it makes sense? How am I supposed to put all of this together and sell products and programs? How am I supposed to put this together and sell the services I provide? AAAAAH, you scream!

I know that you are struggling in business and just trying to make it- period. You understand there is something powerful going on but you can't connect the dots. You see chaos and there is no order to it. You want to deliver a message but you don't know where to start. Now you are in search for some concrete answers of how to monetize your knowledge, wisdom in this cloud called www. buzzzz.com.

On one hand you are excited that you were zapped and on the other hand you are confused. On one hand you were zapped and given this mystical power to connect with people on the other islands called India and China (which has more them 10 times the population of your island USA). You know you can connect with any island and target any audience you desire in the World. You even believe that with this www.bzzzt.com, the Internet, you can communicate with aliens and even sell them what you have. But you don't quite know how to put this CHAOS in order.

For this you need to be zapped one more time. The first zap gave you the power but this zap is going to help you put it all together.

One way you can get zapped, by me, is to attend my academy Sell Like Crazy Academy and The Evolution of an Expert. This is where we help you build products and a program, put together sequences and use the Internet to make profits in the new era. Our promise is that in the days we are together you will walk away with something in your hands. Not just materials but potentially a full product. In our one- two day Sell Like Crazy Academy we help you understand how everything works. But our Evolution Of An Expert; four - five day events are built to help you with actual implementation of the products and services that you want and need. If you would like to learn more, just visit www.FinancialChakras.com

Let me now give you my secret formula so you can build the campaign you were looking to build.

As I said earlier, I came in the financial industry in 1994 at the age of 21. I struggled for seven years in business. I could not close any deals. One of the reasons was that I had not yet figured out MY way of marketing. What I discovered later is that marketing and sales are direct results of adding value strategically to your audience and then asking for the sale. I noticed this formula worked offline first in the 1990's when the Internet came in 2000's and now I am using it on the net and it works on the net just as well.

The formula goes like this:

VVVSUDV or VVVVSVVVV

V. Add Value and get them to fall in love with you, your product and/or your service. Many experts say you have to get your clients to like and trust you, but the reality is today's consumer is not easily attracted with just like and trust. You have to get them to fall in love with you because their pockets are not deep. They are struggling and saving so they can come out easily on the other side.

V. This time give them valuable content they can use. Don't just give them any old boring stuff. Give them content that actually makes sense and gets them to go, "I would have paid money for that."

V. Give them a total reason why they should move forward with you. Give them everything you have.

S. This time summarize the benefits of everything you have sent them, give them an additional unexpected bonus and give them an offer they can't refuse.

This formula changed my life offline and now with online business. It has helped me close 357% bigger transactions then the industry average.

I taught this to Jane Crause, Elanie and Jo Allen. Trust me it works! Go to the next page and build your own **VVVS.**

NOTES

You may be asking "how can I build my own formula?"

Here it is:

- 1st determine how many value pieces you need to add in order to sell your product or service? Hint: The bigger the sale the more value pieces you must add. Whether it is online or offline, it doesn't matter. In general, if the product is selling for around $100 or so one value piece, $100 to $1,000 two-three value pieces, and more than $1,000 three value pieces.

- Circle One

  o   VVVSUDV

  o   VSVSVS

  o   VVVSVVV

  o   VVVVSVVVV

- 2nd Now determine how are you going to add value in each piece. This is determined by first: what is the end result you want your prospect to take? And then what steps will naturally get them there? Hint: A great question I ask is, "How would I get there?"

I want my client to take the following action steps at the end?

_____

_____

I will add the following values to my clients.

_____

_____

_____

_____

- 3rd **Now determine the modality by which you are going to add value to your clients.**

Circle One

O   Video

O   In person one-on-one appointment

O   Seminar

4th Now sell it to them. Note: This should be a natural conclusion to your client's problems. What is the natural conclusion for your clients?

_____

_____

_____

_____ _____

Chapter Six

Sales & Revenue

- How many times have you wondered or felt nervous because you couldn't figure out how to close that deal?

- How many times have you felt like you were on a roller coaster ride?

- How many times have you felt that you were willing and able to help people but they weren't acting on it fast enough?

- How many times did you wonder, "Do I have to be a pushy sales person? Because, that is not who I am?"

Well, you are in luck; you don't have to wonder any longer.

You are going to learn about the three Chakras of Sales. These chakras, if applied properly, whether you are doing online sales or offline sales, can make the desired size transaction. You will be able to make the people buzz and go, "please take me as your client." Please, I know you are not taking any more clients but can you take me? This is the reaction of clients when you do your grunt work of having a dream, picking your target audience, having a world-class marketing system to go after those audiences. Whether you are doing online business or offline business, the formula is universal. How you use it is the difference between industry to industry.

I have used this sales formula for many years and I have been able to close 357% bigger transactions than the industry average.

When I struggled for seven years and it was brutal. I would go on five to twenty appointments a week and I could not close any deals. I would go to these people's houses and give this well-taught and thought out presentation, but every single time it would be a disappointment. I would come home excited but deep down I knew I was not going to make any money. This got so bad that I could not face my family. There were days when I felt depressed. At the same time I am a fighter so I would go at it one more time on a daily basis. I would pick up that "thousand-pound phone" and call one more time and set more appointments. I would go out one more time prospecting for new clients. I would dive in the "hot pool" one more time. I would muster up the courage one more time and go on those appointments, face disappointments and still...come home broke.

You can do this for a while and trust me this gets old, tiring, and depressing. When this happens your self-worth goes to zero and perhaps, even negative. You start doubting everything you do and eventually you may become mentally paralyzed. You know you want to move forward but you can't because you have these pre-conceived notions from your past of the failures you have experienced and they stay with you for a long time. This continues until you decide that it is time to create a break-through, until you decide that it is time for me to strategize before I take action again. That is exactly what I did.

After struggling for seven years, I decided that I am not going to go on an appointment and come home empty handed. So I started searching for who I was? Who I work with best? How can I attract that ideal client using my strength? These are just some of the things I did but the most important thing I did was to go back to my roots; then I saw something that was truly amazing. I thought hmm, what if, just what if I could take this and see how it applies in life and business. Sure enough this worked. It worked so well that I have been able to close 357% bigger transactions then my industry average.

- **I have taught this to ACM Insurance agency, in Elkton MD and they closed $300,000 in deals in just three months. They also built over $1,000,000 in their pipeline.**

- **I taught this to a painting contractor and she closed a $50,000 deal in just two weeks.**

- **I taught this to a carpet cleaning company and they went from $300,000 to over $1,500,000 in just one year.**

- **Recently, I taught this to a new insurance agent. He could not close a deal so I taught him my formula and voila, he closed his first deal in just a week. If that was not enough, he used my seminar presentation technique and had 80% more people come up to him and say, "I would like to sit down with you."**

What I am about to teach you has that type of impact. What I am teaching you has lifelong change. It has changed my life, these people's lives and I am convinced that it will change your life too.

So let me give you the formula first so you can see how it applies throughout this chapter.

There are two main components of sales chakras. One side is about business. The second one is about your prospects' decision-making process.

Let's begin with the business side of chakras:

The Heart of Sales is prospecting

- Make sure you are enjoying the people you work with and enjoy the prospecting method you choose to implement.

- Know your numbers inside and out on a daily, weekly, and monthly basis.

- Number of people you met

- Number of people showed up at your seminars

- Number of people you called

- Number of e-mails you sent

- Number of social media attempts you made

Head of sales are the numbers

- Number of appointments you went on

- Number of sales made per prospects you are seeing

- Number of referrals you obtained from that client

The Gut of Sales is the revenue:

- How much revenue did you generate from one sale?

- What is your target sales revenue per transaction vs. what you made?

- Are you on target to achieve your goals?

You see this is what I didn't understand when I got started. The first side of business is the numbers behind the scenes. I went prospecting blind, without a niche or a marketing plan. To make matters worse I didn't even track these efforts. I was only doing activities. I never followed the path of stopping and evaluating whether or not the path I was following was working for me or not? I simply thought, hey if you go and prospect and talk to anyone you think is a good prospect, that would have been it. All I concentrated on was filling up the calendar with just a bunch of activities and no strategy. I had no particular market or a plan so I just got up in the morning and got busy. What the heck do I know? I am just a 21 year old kid running on adrenalin, the high dosage of convention, and manager's meetings on a weekly basis. All I was told was that you had to meet the people and eventually you will close deals. I did just that. I met a bunch of people and hoped that I would close a deal or two. I prospected my friends, family, and strangers. I did not track the number of appointments, but to make matters worse, I did not even stop to think about me not closing deals, wasting gas, or even my time. Instead I did the opposite. I got more aggressive prospecting and put no strategy in place. I just kept going at it like the "fly on a window." You know what happens to the fly trying to get through the window, right? They die.

Does this sound familiar? Do you see the problem? Go ahead and say it, "what a dummy!" I mean who in the world just wakes up and goes after undecided audience members? Who in the world would just go in the fight blind? Well I have to say duh... me. Yah ME! Ha Ha Ha.... that's funny and flat out stupid. As a matter of fact, it's insane.

Thank God I am not that fly who died.

Knowing what I did wrong and what did not work, helped me plan for the future. That is why when I started my own business and this time I was determined to take my time to evaluate the past, plan my future in a step-by-step manner and develop a system that is beneficial to me and to my clients. The questions I asked myself were:

1. How big did I want to get?

2. Who am I going to target?

3. How am I going to target them?

4. What marketing methods I am going to use?

5. How am I going to use it?

6. How many people am I going to see?

7. How many appointments am I going to generate?

8. How much revenue am I going to generate per transaction?

9. How many transactions am I going to make?

10. How am I going to make this into perpetual marketing and sales?

Internalizing and creating an unfaultable system by which my clients can obtain their goals and dreams, their aspirations and desires, I made sure that I appeal to their likes and avoided their dislikes. I created a system and choose specific ways of serving my audience which was proven to work and I believed in it one thousand percent. I choose this system because that is how I would like to be taken care of and that is how I have invested my parents' money safe and sound.

That brings us to the second component, which is the prospects' decision-making process.

How do prospects make decisions?

To create clients you need the following three main chakras to gain clients and not just customers:

1. Love

You must get your prospects to fall in love with you.

How?

Have fun with your prospect. Don't be a stiff pole or a stick in the mud. Just relax and be yourself.

Get your prospect in an environment that is safe and secure for you and for them. For instance, I like to get people in seminars and have a great time with them. Then I would have an intimate conversation about their likes, dislikes, wants, and needs at their kitchen table. Some people like to meet the prospects one-on-one across the kitchen table right from the get go. I like wining and dining with people but some people like non-public environments. The bottom-line is to choose an environment that is going to be relaxing and have an intimate conversation. The most important part is that you choose an environment that is going relaxing for you and the prospect.

Discuss their concerns and aspirations.

This is the key at the end of the day. Prospects are looking for someone that can say, "Hey, I can help you and here is how." Stake your claim. My claim has always been "Ash Protects Cash 100% of the time." I have not only said this but also built a business that helped people lose zero dollars in the 2008 crash. I have people telling me this over and over again.

2. Intelligence

You must appeal to your prospects intellectually. They must go, "hmm that makes sense." How?

...by letting them know honestly if what they are doing currently is good or not.

...by giving them some hints and logical reasons to move along with you.

When I go on my first and second appointments, my purpose is not to sell but to build rapport and give them a "30,000 foot view" of their finances, along with some "golden nuggets" that would help them. The purpose of these two appointments is to further the conversation and not to sell. The purpose of these appointments is to make sure you are having a conversation of what is important to them and give them a "30,000 foot view" of their finances. One more thing, drop hints in as to where you are looking to take them and how. Watch for their reaction if they love your suggestions then you are on the right path. If not, change the course and get it to more of their liking. This is what I do and did after finding my groove. Trust me; your prospects will love you for this.

3. Intuition

Execution of your solution must hit a home run. It has to fulfill the need, wants, and ambition. It should also help them abandon their fears. All these bases must be covered.

How?

Give them an unshakable reason why they should work with you. When I go on my third appointment, I know exactly what they like and love. I have revised their plan and now it is the time for me to present the final plan. But you see by now they have fallen in love with who I am, and what I say appeals to them intelligently. The third piece is to show them what we have been discussing so far. Give them the plan of their liking and make sure that upon execution, you take care of your clients. Make sure they know and you know that after implementing your solution they will be better off, their lives will transform and their world will change forever. Usually I have to meet the prospects a 4th time to do the paperwork and that is the way I like it. The reason I choose it to be this way is because I don't want any doubt in their mind that what I am doing is the best solution for them. I don't want any anxiety in their mind about their financial future. I want to eliminate their doubts and fears and replace them with hope and aspirations. But most importantly create an unbreakable bond.

NOTE: As my client and a friend if you want to discuss your finances I would be happy to help you in any way I can. Just shoot me an e-mail or call me at my office.

So now it is time for the report card. Does this really work Ash? This is the question I get from people all the time. Listen, I have been able to close 357% higher transactions then the industry average. I have taught this to others and they too have received fantastic results.

An insurance agency took their sales from zero to $300,000 and developed one million dollar in the pipeline in just three months.

A painting contractor closed a $50,000 deal in just two weeks.

Listen, use this process in any way you can and it will give you amazing results. The beauty of this process is that it works in any situation. If you are making big transactions, meet with your prospects several times. If you are making small transactions, then the time spent becomes shortened. But you should follow all four steps to create clients and not just customers.

Online Sales

The previous paragraphs were about offline sales. Ash, you may ask, what about online sales? What about those social media, website, and e-mail marketing tools? What can we do with that? How can we make sales online?

You are in luck! I am going to discuss that as well. Let's cover the basics first.

What is an Internet sale? Internet sales are known as "sales funnels." So think about a series of marketing campaigns that add value to your target audience and then finally you get to ask for the sale. This sounds familiar, doesn't it? Offline sales are not that different from online sales. The problem is that perhaps you have not mastered one, so the other one looks more difficult than it actually is. Do yourself a favor, master one so well that no one can beat you on it and then go to the next because they are about the same. The difference is one is in person and other one is on the "net. "

I know you are thinking, "But which medium should I choose?" How do I know what is good for me? Relax let me tell you the basics first.

There are ten main mediums of marketing:

1.   Facebook

2.   Twitter

3.   LinkedIn

4.   YouTube

5.   Vimeo

6.   Kajabi

7. Your website

8. E-Mail

9. Shopping cart (Infusion Soft)

10. Mobile Apps

So how does this work and how can you put it all together? Think of all of these as a medium to hit different chakras. These mediums help you achieve different results.

Facebook and Twitter should be used for making friends and authenticate who you are. The mistake people make is that they try to sell all the time on these mediums. These mediums are great for promotions, creating brand awareness, **but mostly I use them for just being there to connect with people in a human way.** These mediums are great for creating a following that is unsurpassable.

Facebook

What else is Facebook great for, you ask? Well here is how I use it, sometimes as an appointment setting tool. Usually around 9:00-11:00 at night, let's say I have been trying to get in touch with this person XYZ and I just can't connect. What I do is to get on Facebook late at night and see on the right side of the screen if that person has a green dot. If they have a green dot that means they are there and I can open a chat. Where I say, "hi" and set up an appointment that way.

Video Chat on Facebook

Ok, Ash, but I hear people are making money on Facebook. How do they do it? How do you make money on Facebook? Can you please tell me what else Ash? Facebook is great for business but how do you use it? This may be a surprise to you, but did you know you can do a video chat? This is the BOMB! Woo hoo, yes, yes, oh, yes. This is the Buzzz factor. This is the zap factor. Check out how I use it. Let's say I want to connect with someone in India and I want to connect with a face-to-face meeting. So what I do is turn on Facebook and have them do the same. Then on the bottom right hand side where there are green dots I find the person I want to do a video call with. I click on their name or picture and a chat box pops up. In the chat box there is a video button. Just click and it will call the other person instantly. When the person accepts a call this way, you can talk to the person like a face-to-face appointment. By using this tool I have closed so many sales it's not even funny. The best part is, it is FREE. YES, aha, aha, aha, aha. Yes, aha, aha, aha, aha. Cha-ching! is the word that comes to my mind. Just make sure you take your prospects through the three-appointment process I discussed earlier. That is it and you can make money on Facebook.

There is only one caution on this one. Make sure you are dressed professionally and your background is neat. Dress professional, DON'T SPEAK WITH YOUR PROSPECT IN YOUR PJ's! This is a NO, NO, NO. You are guaranteed to lose the sale.

Twitter

I use it just as a mechanism tool to help me communicate with the audience in a small burst of messages. Also, it is a great tool if you use hash tags (a hash tag is the number symbol #) for tracking your seminar attendees or anything you want for that matter. I think you should do the same.

LinkedIn

While Facebook and Twitter are more personal connection sites, LinkedIn is a great professional connection site. This is great, especially if your target market is business owners and professionals. LinkedIn can be used in many different ways. One way you can use it is just by creating connections with other professionals. Another way I use it is to promote events I have coming up and send personal e-mail messages that connects with a prospect or potential prospect. I always use this medium when I want to target a specific industry or geographical location. By using this tool, I am able to promote it to my target audience.

YouTube and Vimeo

These are the two largest video platforms for you to market your company, brand, and product. How can you use it? You and I know that videos are being watched more than ever before. How you can use it to optimize your site? Take 10 videos and post them on these channels. Videos one, two, and three and use them to tell who you are and how you can help your clients in a minute or less. Videos four, five, six and seven, use them to answer any pressing questions that your clients have. Videos eight, nine, and ten, use them to overcome your clients' concerns. This is the secret of internet marketers. They have figured this out. They have deliberately put together ways to communicate with you which make you want to go; "I need that." Isn't that cool?

Kajabi

What? What is Kajabi? You have heard the phrase "building landing pages," haven't you? Well that is what Kajabi helps you do. I use Kajabi for all my videos and landing pages. What is cool about Kajabi is that you can build a landing page the way you want it, the way you see fit. You can do text or video, you can do this on any landing page platform. The coolest part is that it is easy to use and social media driven. The best part is you can build online courses. You can build funnels and projects.

Your website

Is your website effective? Most people think of website as a credibility tool. But the most effective use of a website is information gathering tool. Hmm... you say. Yes, think about it. What is your real estate in business today? Your database and connections are your real estate. That is why the first thing you need to have is an opt-in form on the front page of your website site. The second thing you need are videos. The third thing you need is a chronological order of actions that you want your prospects to take. If your goal is to close the prospect in buying your product or service, then there needs to be an order of content. The most important thing you **must** have on your website is you, your personality, and your brand. If you don't have this you will have an incredibly hard time in business today.

E-Mail Addresses

Let me stress the importance of this. You must have these. Do you want to know the secret to the Internet marketers in making a million dollars per year? Their database. Yes! Their database. So how big of a database do you need to make a million dollars? 10,000 names and e-mail addresses. "What?" you said, "that is it?" Yes, if you have 10,000 e-mail addresses and you add constant value to those people on a weekly or monthly basis. You can and will have a million dollar business. That is sick isn't it? The question is... will you make this your focus?

Personal challenge: Get 10,000 e-mail addresses

in one year. Send me e-mail to

Ash@AshIsCash.com let me know your progress and when you reach your target. Then I will give you two FREE tickets to my Sell Like Crazy Academy Online and Live Academy valued at $2,000.

Shopping Cart

People ask me all the time which shopping cart should I use? And I say you can use whichever kind you want but I use **Infusion soft**. I use this shopping cart for several reasons:

1. It is a one-stop business-building tool for me.

2. It is easy to use.

3. It has Customer Relationship Manager (CRM) and a shopping cart built in. You can also look at: **One Shopping Cart,** as well, if you would like to see another option.

Mobile Apps

Now this is the future coming along with videos. So pay attention. You must consider getting your mobile app in the near future. You must master this part of the game as well. My mobile app is AshIsCash and FinancialChakras on Android and iPhone. With this, you can send out push notifications and instant messages, opt in pages and videos. You can have anything imaginable, but the most important thing that you must have in your app. This is the reason for your prospect to use your app.

Now the question is how do you do VVVSUDV or VVVVSVVVV on the internet? How do you hit the chakras and close that deal? Let me help you make sales online. First off, understand that making sales online is not that much different than offline sales. It is essentially the same. The main difference is that now you have to choose a communication device that works for you.

Three chakras of Internet marketing:

The Heart Chakra: The medium you choose must match your personality and you must come through as though you are there in person with them.

The Head Chakra: You must communicate messages that are intriguing and intellectually stimulating.

The Gut Chakra: You must have a message that resonates with them throughout your campaign. You must have a message that takes them to the point of buying in a step 1, step 2, etc.

This is how I do this. I choose videos as my medium. Because some time ago I figured out that I work best when I can be seen in groups and give seminars. To accomplish this online, I use video marketing. I use **Kajabi**, my website, and Infusion Soft to close my audience.

Why do I do this? Kajabi helps me upload the videos, market my message, and make it go viral. It also serves as a lead-gathering tool. Which means I can choose to show an opt-in page or not. It's completely up to me. My purpose is to have people share the actual videos and as they share, gather names, e-mails and phone numbers, I build my real estate.

My website helps me build my list further, it helps me build my brand and credibility, but the most important thing is that it helps me sell my products and programs.

Infusion Soft is where I create the magic. This is not just a CRM system but it is also a central location for names, e-mails, and phone numbers. I can create campaigns, tag individuals, groups, and organizations and track where the prospect is from. It can Track revenue and most importantly cultivate my list in a way that makes them fans and followers. I can do this by building an e-mail campaign and insert links to the videos from Kajabi.

For social media, my purpose of Facebook, Twitter, and LinkedIn is to just connect with people and constantly remind them that, "hey, don't forget I am here to help." As far as an advertisement, I like LinkedIn for ads.

Now you put together a campaign for yourself.

Here is what you need to do:

- Decide where you want your prospects to end up. How do they like to learn, video or text?

- Decide the hurdles that your prospects face in the journey to your desired outcome.

- Help them overcome those hurdles and make it easy for them go get to the destination, your product or service.

Now let's choose the mediums and put them in chronological order:

1.   Create an opt-in page using your e-mail provider.

2. Decide which vehicle you are going to use to drive massive value to your audience.

3. Be sure to pick a vehicle that matches your personality. To do this, go back in history of what you have done and what you enjoy the most. If you like talking to people face-to-face, choose video. If you are shy and an introvert then choose just text e-mails. As far as conversions, video converts much better than text.

4. Decide which medium you are going to choose to drive the value and help them overcome the hurdles. Is it e-mails or social media?

5. If it is e-mails, then go with a program that delivers automatic e-mails.

6. Once you have added value to your prospects, now it is time to sell them.

Ok, how can you do that? Let me give you a full format of how to create an online sales video or a sales letter.

Heart

Promise your prospect what they are going to accomplish

Head

Build your credibility and what it takes to win

It's a comprehensive program that they can learn from

Gut

Why are you doing it?

- Describe the entire module and everything they are going to learn

- Great guarantee and price

- Great call to action

You may be looking at this and going "Uh, what should I do? This sales stuff is difficult." Yes, it is, but I promise it gets easier as you do it. Start the exercises because that is the only way you are going to learn. I had to do it, others had to do it, and now it's your turn. The good news is you have a formula and we did not.

There is nothing to be afraid of. Fear is the reason most people don't take any action. But this making the sale stuff is easy. All you have to do is follow the format. Will you make mistakes along the way? Will you stumble? YES and YES. But think about it. When was the last time you learned something without mistakes? So why would you be afraid now? So go ahead and give it a shot.

If you want, I can help you a little further. All you have to do is attend my Sell Like Crazy Academy. Where we not only teach you all of this, but help you implement this on the spot. You and your friends can register at www.FinancialChakras.com.

NOTES

Let's begin with the business side of chakras:

Who is your target audience?

_____

_____

How many prospects are you going to see on a weekly, monthly, and yearly basis? _____

How much revenue would you like to earn per week, month, and year?

_____

How will you get your prospect to fall in love with you?

_____

_____

_____

_____

How will you appeal to your prospect's intelligence?

_____

_____

_____

_____

_____

_____
_____
_____
_____

How will you appeal to their intuition?

_____
_____
_____
_____
_____

What will your closing sequence looks like?

_____
_____
_____
_____
_____
_____
_____

How will you deliver Heart, Head, and the Gut presentation?

_____
_____
_____
_____

How are you going to structure your offline and online chakras and sales chakras?

_____

_____

_____

_____

_____

_____

_____

_____

_____

_____

_____

_____

_____

_____

_____

_____

_____

_____

_____

_____

_____

_____

_____

_____

Chapter Seven

Evolution Of An Expert

As I speak from location to location, I have found is that most businesses are suffering in this economy. They are wondering:

1. How can I generate more revenue?

2. How can I earn more and have the lifestyle of my dreams?

3. How can I position my business better in the marketplace?

These are just some of the questions that go through your head when you are trying to make it in today's economy.

In a desperate attempt to make it, you hear someone say you need to be the expert in your field. You need to write that book, or have products and programs. You may say, "Oh, yeah, that's right, that is exactly correct." So you go on this quest of building your product and program. In your excitement you write the introduction of your book and you write the first and the second chapters but then life gets in the way. A day, a week, a month, sometimes years pass because you did not take the time to understand - why you need to be the expert. How can you become the go-to expert? How can this benefit you in the short run and in the long run? Since you don't see the full picture you get caught in this hype of becoming the go-to expert.

That is exactly why I am writing this chapter. This chapter is designed to help you understand how this works and how can you turn becoming the go-to expert into revenue.

What is an expert? An expert is someone who shares his or her ideas, knowledge, or wisdom in a way that helps others who are in search for better results. Do you have knowledge about a subject matter that would help someone? Can you draw a roadmap and lay out the steps for someone to go from Point A to Point B? Can you do the research or interview someone that can give their input on how to do XYZ in order for you to teach that to others? If you answered "yes" then congratulations! Now you can be the go-to expert in your field.

Do you know the following people?

§   Tony Robbins

§   Brendon Burchard

§   Brian Tracy

§   Napoleon Hill

§   Zig Ziglar

These guys weren't experts when they started. As a matter of fact, they were completely broke. What they understood were three chakras of becoming the expert.

Chakra #1 The Heart Chakra:

Why should you become the go-to expert in your respective field?

When you look at these guys, it is almost intimidating to see the fact that these guys are making all of this money. The first two gentlemen, alone bring in about forty million dollars. That is amazing, you say! But what you don't see is what drives them to the best at what they do and why they do it. I will tell you that it is not the forty million dollars that drives them at all. Almost no one sees the hard work and determination that goes behind their work. No knows it, but them. That's because they don't mind the hard work they love what they do. These guys are on a mission to change the world for the better. They are determined to do everything they can to change people's lives. They don't have this fluffy idea but they executed that idea and took the risk to be in business of changing others' lives for the better. They dove into the business of helping us and change our lives. They did this because they were sick and tired of their lives being the same old -same old. They decided to do this because they saw no other alternative. They made up their minds and said "I had enough of this" and then decided to tell their story of struggle in such an elegant way that it captivated you. Then they asked ok how could I hang out with everyone at the same time? So to do this they built products and programs. That is how they gained popularity. At last they were able to sell what they knew to be valuable and make money from it. But I am venturing to say that the real value that they received was not monitory compensation. The real value was the satisfaction that they received from their work, such as the satisfaction of helping others. Satisfaction of creating something that made a difference. Having the satisfaction of creating a world-class product. Satisfaction of discovering who they are and what they can achieve if they put their minds to it. And lastly, proving to themselves and they said, "Hey, look I can make it in this world. I am someone. I am the best and you can bet by coming to me, that I will drive you to results."

When I got started in the financial services business I had no credibility. I just did my mundane tasks of talking to people, setting appointments, and giving presentations. But the fact was that they did not see this twenty one year old kid as an expert. They were not ready to hand me their money. That was one reason that I struggled in business. I did not have any books, CDs, DVDs or anything else for that matter. Can you imagine this dork in front of 40, 50, 60 year olds asking if they want to invest their hard earned money with him? No, of course not! Looking back I can see that I didn't have skills, knowledge and the ability of becoming the go-to expert by writing that book and positioning myself as the go-to expert. I did not know how to build products and programs to be considering an expert. This was a major factor for me to getting any business; I simply didn't have the credibility. Let me tell you though what happens when you do gain the knowledge and become the go-to expert. Once I understood the fact that I had to become the expert, I wrote three books and my credibility went through the roof. Those who said no to me initially now come and ask me for my help because I have the credibility and I am the go-to expert in my field. This has happened to me several times. People come up to me on a regular basis and ask me all the time, "Can you take care of our money?" They literally give me hundreds of thousands of dollars. As a matter of fact, this happened to me just two weeks ago were my dad's friend came to me and said, "can you help me invest the money I have, and put it into a safe vehicle?" And now we are going to plan his retirement with almost $400,000. I have sold the book that you are reading, before I even finished it AND made money from it. I have been honored to have spoken at congressional conferences, all from becoming the expert. As a result of becoming the go-to expert, I get invited to business groups and teach them how to build their multi- million dollar empire. If that is not enough, I get thousands of dollars to coach someone. So what types of programs do I have, you ask? I have a one day Sell Like Crazy Academy, DVDs, online programs, CDs, and, of course, this book. You may be thinking you want to do this because you can make lots of money and get rich beyond your wildest dreams. The real reason and the main purpose of building products and programs is to leave a legacy in the world. So when you are gone from the earth you can still live on this earth. There are side benefits of building your products and programs, such as raising instant credibility, being able to earn more by charging more, and creating a secondary online recurring revenue source. The biggest benefit though, is the knowledge that you will gain by doing the research and the pride you feel when you have your own products and programs. By developing your materials you will be able articulate your message better, and become an effective communicator. You can become the best coach in your subject matter.

The best part is the satisfaction you will have in helping others and living the legacy even after you are gone. Ok, that is all good, but give me all the reasons I should become the expert in my field. Let me be more specific about how becoming an expert can change your life.

Earning more money: You want to earn $100,000

Scenario 1: Let's say that you are a business owner who is struggling to earn money in these tough economic times. You are working 90 hours per week and can't seem to get anywhere. To grow your business the only alternative is apply and teach what you know. So you decide to do the modalities below and gain the expert status so that your clients can see that this is the person or company I should do business with because they are clearly the experts.

Scenario 2: You are a boomer who is worried about your retirement income. You have saved money in your retirement all these years and now it is time for you to retire but you feel you still need to do something because you might run out of money. In addition, you are looking for alternative ways to earn money so you can keep your retirement savings intact.

Special NOTE: If you are a business owner who needs help in building their business, but are on a limited budget, I have a monthly program where we get together for an hour on a conference call, webinar, video, or live webcast on a weekly basis. If you miss a session, don't worry they are recorded. Visit www. FinancialChakras.com for details.

If you are worried about your retirement, I can help you there too. I have helped many families successfully put together plans on how not to run out of money at old age. I have shown people how not to lose money in any market condition. As a matter of fact in the 2008 crash, my clients lost zero dollars. So if you are concerned about your retirement in any way shape or form, about outliving it or losing it in the market, just give me a call and I will offer you the guidance that you need. Here is my number 410-493-3358 and my e-mail is Ash@FinancialChakras.com

So if you are a business owner or a boomer, here is how you can earn $100,000 in this field:

- Write a book that sells for $19.99. All you would have to do is sell 5002 books per year or 417 books per month.

- Hold monthly webinar which you charge $49. All you would have to do is sell 2041 for the entire year or sell 171 per month.

- Offer a membership sites where you just charge $97 per month. All you would need to do is get just 87 clients for life and you are done.

What if you are a boomer and looking for an alternative way to retire wouldn't this be awesome? This alone would give you a $8,333/month in income.

- DVD program: Let's say you charge $497. Did you know that all you would need to sell is 201 sets for the year and just 17 sets per month?

- Let's say that you built an online course which you sell for $2,000. All you need to sell is 50 courses per year or just 4.2 courses per month.

- Let's say you have a monthly coaching program which you charge $2,000 per month to a client. All you would need is 8.3 clients for life and you are done.

- Speeches @$10,000. All you would have to do is book 10 speaking engagements.

YES! Ash YES! I am excited to earn this money but Ash; I don't know how to build products and programs. No worries I have a class called Evolution of an Expert where we bring you in and help you build products and programs on the spot. To find the course send me an e-mail at

Ash@FinancialChakras.com or visit www.FinancialChakras.com.

But for now let me get you started on how to become the go to expert.

Chakra #2 The Head Chakra

How to become an expert?

I have talked to so many people who care deeply about what they do and tell me all the time how much difference they want to make in the world. They want to raise their credibility in their prospects' eyes so that they can earn more and work less by charging more. They want to have the recurring revenue online and offline. But the single biggest reason they can't is that they don't have anything to sell. They always seem to get stuck on creating products and programs. Are you in this situation? Do you want to make a difference, earn more, and grow consistently? I totally understand that, because I have been there. And now I reveal the secret you have been waiting to hear.

Basically becoming the expert is pretty simple. All you have to do is figure out how you are going to be the expert. There are three ways to becoming an expert:

1. Become the results expert

Basically all you are doing is showing your audience, who is trying to get to where you are, a path from point A to point B. For instance, I am teaching you how to build your multi-million dollar empire, by either reading this book, attending my Sell Like Crazy Academy, buy my online course, buy my CDs, DVDs or get involved in our monthly program.

2. Become the research expert

When I got started speaking and training I was thinking about a subject I can speak on. In my research I thought about Mount Everest as a metaphor to be used as business building. I was going to use what I know, and what I had researched on how business owners succeed and teach that in a way that would have a zing to it. I studied businesses and Mount Everest and combined the two and decided going to speak about it.

3.   You are the Role Model

People ask advice from people they love, trust, and respect.

Think about it: Have you ever listened to your mom, dad, neighbor, best buddy, a friend even though they know nothing about ......? To become this kind of expert, all you have to do is become engaged in their life, that's it!

Now with all of this said and done, you are wondering, but Ash how do you write that darn book, or make all of these products and programs? Ok.

Let me give you three chakras of building a product or a program:

1.   The Heart chakra is for **any** product or **program that is your story** or another's story, if you don't have one.

2.   The Head chakra for this is showing the future and showing your audience the path of going from point A to point B, and showing them the specific steps that they can implement. For instance, I am showing you your five steps to building your multi-million dollar empire.

3.   The Gut chakra is where you get paid. If you are wondering why you are not getting paid, this is the reason. This is where Tony Robbins, Brendon Burchard, Zig Ziglar and many others who shine because they can take the most complex systems and break them down so

you not only learn about, it but can be implemented it in your life. Most people tell you that you need to build your own products and programs but they don't tell you how. They sell on the dream of making millions but they can't tell you how to earn just $100,000 in the most-simple form possible. You see this is where the great ones differ and my goal is to help you differentiate yourself without being a copycat, that way you too can achieve that level of success. You, must show in your program, how to get the desired solution your audience is seeking. For me it is about helping you build your multi-million dollar empire.

This is Ash's secret formula for building any product or program:

Let's build a product shall we?

The product we are going to build is writing your book.

Heart

1. What is the audience you want to serve?

2. What is the message you want to drive?

3. What are the results you want them to accomplish?

Head

1.   Decide three to five stories of your life, which has pain and pleasure.

Pick one story that you would like to tell the most. Hint: Pick a story of pain. Caution: pick a story that will take them from point A to point B. Meaning if you know about XYZ matter, then the story needs to be about the pain and/or struggle while getting there and what was the pleasure. I met a lady who is great at corporate strategic planning and she is brilliant at event marketing for corporations. However, the problem is she wasn't able to figure out how she put together a multi-million dollar mind map, strategic plans, and put together marketing campaigns that gets eight thousand people at an event. I asked her to tell me the story and as she told the story I brought out the bullet points how she was doing this. I am telling you my story about how I built my empire from zero to multi-million dollars and what five steps I took to get there. Your story must have a pain and pleasure. Hint: higher pain = higher readership.

2.   Take them on a journey. So what you do is just think what you did to get to where you are. Now break them down in 3 - 5 - 7 - 10 steps.

3.   Teach them how to avoid problems on their way to... and implement the solutions right away.

Allow me to show you what I am doing in this book. I told you about who I am and what my struggles have been. Then I told you that in search of answers after spending over 12,000 hours and over $110,000 in self-improvement I ended up with a rocking business. In my search I learned five important concepts and how I mastered them with a message that if you do these things, you too can get to where I am. The kicker is the last part where I not just told you, but showed you what mistakes I made, that way, you can avoid them. The solutions that I discovered that worked and then how to implement those solutions to help you grow your business. This is true for all of these successful entrepreneurs who have made millions. It's the same formula.

You can build any product or program you like using this formula and you can make a ton of money doing it!

I know what you are thinking but what programs can I build and how can I build my empire doing it? There are so many different things I can build. Where do I start? Which one should I build first? How can I put them in order that makes sense? How can I earn money?

Chakra# 3 The Gut chakra: So how do you build a multi-million dollar empire by becoming the go-to expert in your field?

Here is how it works.

Decide on one product you are going to build.

Decide what that product is used for. Is the product designed to help you gain credibility so you can sell your services easier? Or is your product the end game? If the product is the end game then think about what the ultimate product is that you are trying to sell.

I have seen many people fail in this area; they want to be the author, speaker, and trainer. They want to become this big business person and gain fame. So they rush and make a rash decision. Which leads to failure. Instead, doesn't it make sense to stop and think about your steps before you make them and then map out a plan? That is how I think. In 2004 what I discovered is that by writing books I can gain credibility and crush the competition. And surely enough I did. I would be sitting at networking events and hearing the other guys talking about how I talk about the same thing as they do, in my book. But almost always people wanted to deal with me rather than the other person. Why was that? As I am writing this book and people have heard about it. Do you know what was happening? People began asking me to come and do the speaking engagements. They want to put together my academy and rock the house.

So what is the difference you ask? In my financial practice I used books as a leveraging tool. In my Ash Is Cash business, I help business owners and entrepreneurs earn more cash. In this business I built a suite of products for me to get paid. So what types of products can you really build?

Here are the lists of products you can build:

1. Books

2. E-Books

3. Teleseminars

4. Audio

5. Webinars

6. Continuity/membership

7. Speeches

8. Seminars

9. Online

10. DVD programs

11. Coaching & Mastermind Classes

12. Webcasts

Now you see why it is confusing. You have all of these modalities and don't know how to use them all. I would like to share some business information, the goal is to minimize marketing expenses and maximize profits. This is how I used them; you can understand how to use them properly. Seminars, teleseminars, webinars, webcasts, and speeches will become your marketing tools. This is where you get to tell your brief story. These can be 20 to 60 minutes in length.

I use books, e-books, single disk audio and single disk DVD as your low-ticket item. These are easy clutches, which you can either sell or use as promotional material. If you are going to drive to a place and spend your time and money to get there, this is the time you want to bring these items out and sell them from the stage. These items are generally there to cover your cost and gain credibility. Now if your book becomes a best seller Woo Hoo, I am cheering for you that is the best that is not the norm.

Now let's get to the big-ticket items. Multi-disk audios, multi-disk DVDs, online membership programs, continuity program, mastermind and finally coaching programs are sold where you are having in-depth conversations, such as one-on-one meetings; use this as a rule of thumb. Now you can sell any and all of these programs online at any time. However, the higher the price, the more value you have to add up front.

So what should be the price?

1. Books: $19.99 - $49.99

2. E-Books: $9.99

3. Tele seminars: FREE - $49

4. Speeches: FREE in general - $150,000

5. Seminars: FREE - $10,000

6. Webinars: FREE - $197

7. Webcasts: FREE - $297

8. Single-disk audio CD: FREE - $9.99

9. Multi-disk audio CD: $29.99 - $297

10. Single-disk DVD: FREE - $29.99

11. Multi-disk DVD: $49.99 - $597

12. Continuity membership: $97/Month

13. Online: $99 - $5,000

14. Coaching & Mastermind Classes: $500 - $25,000/Month

Now let's see how you can make money from this. Let's assume
that you have these programs. How would the sale look? Well,
you would do the speaking engagement where you did not get
paid to go and speak. Your cost is time and gas. Let's assume that
you time is worth $100 per hour and you spent four hours of your
time. That means you have spent $400. Your target is to walk

away with $400 - $2,000. All you would have to do is combine your book, CD, and DVD which you will sell for just $97. Usually about 30% of the crowd buys the products. That works out to be just 30 people. That means 30 people bought, times $97 that equals $2,910 in up front revenue for one hour of speaking. If you are great, you can sell all 100 people at $97 and you have made a whopping $9,700 dollars. WOW!

Let's take it a step further. Now what happens is that some people want to have relationships with you and go deeper. The percentage of people who want to go deeper is about 20%. So out of 100 let's say you sell 15 people your DVD and CD set for $795. This is equal to $15,900 additional revenue.

But this does not stop here. What happens is that the 20% who would want to contract your personal services simply are not in a position to afford your $10,000 programs. Usually 5% or so over time pays you the $2,000/month. Ok, so that is additional revenue of $10,000/month because out of 100 people you spoke to about five who will engage in the one-on-one trainings.

Now you see why it is so important to develop products and programs. You could get just one speaking engagement and that turns into $2,910 plus $15,900 equal to $18,810 from one speaking engagement. Don't forget you have also picked up five personal coaching clients, which pays you

$2,000/month each totaling $10,000/month. Of course that means you have just built a two million dollar annuity that pays you $120,000/year in residual income.

One more thing that has happened from speaking and that is you may have gotten another speaking engagement, which continues the revenue cycle going.

If you don't have products and programs it is going to be difficult for you to make it. Here is my offer. I have a program called Evaluation of An Expert, which helps you build products and programs on the spot. We generally help people write books, CDs, DVDs and other programs. The beauty is you don't have to worry about anything. We give you the templates and all the work is done for you. All you have to do is fill in the blanks. We will even set up your funnels of adding values, and your systems of how you are going to make money. If you are interested in that give me a call at 410-493-3358 or E-Mail me at Ash@FinancialChakras.com and I will be happy to discuss the details.

So now you see how you could be on a beach relaxing and earning money. By building products and programs you can have your dreams come true. By building a system that pays over and over again is the key to being a millionaire. If you ever wanted to be a millionaire this is your time. This is your time to make a difference in the world. This is your time to build your empire and leave a legacy. This is your time to build your dream. This is your time to be the best you can be and do the best you can do. This is...YOUR TIME. That's right; it's your time to SHINE...RIGHT NOW!

Remember your childhood is gone, your youth is gone, but now it is your time to Charge ahead and live! So sing with me, give me some sunshine, give me some rain and give me another chance because I want to grow up once again. That is the real reason; you need to build your products and programs. To leave your legacy so when you look through those windows from heaven above, you can see how you are living on forever and how your work is making a difference in the world.

It's time for you to build your program so go to the next page and fill out some questions and build your own program.

NOTES

I would build my products for the following audience?

_____

_____

_____

_____

_____

_____

_____

I would like to build the following products?

_____

_____

_____

_____

_____

In a nutshell, my story is...

_____

_____

_____

_____

_____

_____

_____

My story has the following main points.

- _____

- _____

- _____

- _____

- _____

- _____

My story has the following teaching points...

- _____

- _____

- _____

- _____

Other stories I have, are...

- _____

- _____

- _____

- _____

I plan to build my first product by _____.

I want to build my products and programs because...

_____

_____

_____

_____

_____

_____

_____

I want to dedicate my products to _____

I would price my product at _____ price.

To reach $100,000 by selling my product and program, I would have to sell _____ units per year and _____ per month.

I am a creator and I am proud of it! YES / NO

_____

_____

_____

_____

_____

_____

_____

Chapter Eight

Rock their world

Ever since you were born, you have thought about rocking your world. You have always wanted to reach new heights and do something that you are proud of. You have been searching for a formula to succeed in life. You decided to learn new ways of doing things and invested your time and hard earned money in getting better. You may have gone to many seminars, read self-improvement books, CDs and programs. You are working hard to make a difference in the world. Are you trying to rock your clients' world? At the end, you may look down through the windows of heaven and say, "hey look! There is my family. I took a risk, built my empire and now they have the life of their dreams. Look at the second window. I see the non-profit I opened has passed the goal of helping one million people. See that! My friends, neighbors and relatives are all happy for my family because I did something extraordinary. YES! I was a rock star." You are born to make a difference in other people's lives. That is what makes us humans. We want to change the world for the better. We want to leave a legacy, so that even after we are gone, people will talk about us. Believe me, people want heroes! Why can't you be the hero in their world? To do that, is simple. Just rock their world by being passionate about what you do. Be passionate about making a difference in your client's life, understand their wants and needs. Be energetic about what you do. Be compassionate about your clients and their feelings; and don't just meet, but exceed their needs. Go above and beyond for your clients. At the end of the day, if you are here to help and make a difference, you can't help but rock their world. Go make a difference and leave a legacy of your dreams.

Let me share some stories how I like to rock the world.

First, my dream is to go back to the Georgia dome and speak. I want to excite the world by building the largest monument in Washington DC. I have this crazy idea of building the largest flag in the world. Not just any flag, but a human flag. Now can you imagine a sky view of what it would be like to have millions of people between the monument and the Capitol forming a U.S. flag? Now that's what I call rocking it out! I would love to have you at that gathering. I want to rock it out with you. If you want to rock it out with me at the monument feel free to register on my site www.FinancialChakras.com. I also love to rock the world of my clients by helping them earn more money, grow their business or portfolio, and teach them how to keep what they have.

Let's take a look at some of my clients that I have helped.

$50,000 Deal in Just Two Weeks

One day I was speaking at a local community college where a business development center was having an event. After my speech, a young lady came up to me and said, "I am trying to close a deal and this bid is due in few days." She and I spoke for a few minutes. After our conversation, what we discovered was very simple. We both agreed that she needed help. So in her case we put together a strategy using the combination of the sales and marketing segment from this book. You know what happened? She closed a $50,000 deal in just two weeks. She felt like a rock star when she got the check.

$1,000,000 in New Revenue Pipeline

Speaking at the same event the owner of an insurance agency came up to me and said, "We are starting a new division and we need help in building our new life and health division." I decided to take on the challenge. Well, what can I say? After working with them for about three months they closed over $300,000 in business and had over $1,000,000 in a new revenue pipeline.

1,600% Increase in Two Weeks

I love working with boomers and industry peers. I was training a local business group in Rockville, Maryland. One boomer insurance agent, in his 50's came up to me and said, "I just got laid off." He was one of my training attendees. He told me that he didn't want to go to work for someone else ever again. I'll call him BOB. Of course I said, "Congratulations Bob." But let me tell you, I was scared for the guy for many reasons. First, he had no business experience. Second, he had never done sales before. Third, he was using his retirement assets to survive. He then proceeded to tell me that he has bought this amazing system for $6,000 and they gave him everything he needed to sell insurance. So I asked, "What is the system?" The company put together a mailing invitation, which supposedly brings target prospects to him. To top that off, they had put together a seminar, which works for all their guys. Of course these guys made lots of money doing this. I said to Bob, "that is great. How much have you put out so far?" He said he had put out about $20,000 just for mailings. Ok, I thought he must have made about $50,000 if he has spent $20,000 right? So I asked, "How much have you made?" He said, "Zero." Hmm... that's interesting I thought. But then I thought about it. What is the problem? Why is he not making money? The problem was two-fold. First, he did not know about the chakras, more importantly he was doing what everyone does; hit his prospects in the head by unloading information and trying to push his product. He was trying to push products instead of identifying the client needs. He realized he needed help. So he brought me on as a consultant. You know what happened after working with him for about two weeks? He closed his first deal. Though he did not make a killing in his deal but when you go from $0 - $1,600 in two weeks. That is significant. His business went from struggling to 1,600% increase. Not only that, he had a seminar scheduled where he was going to give the same old presentation. I told him to dump that presentation because it was not producing results. We put together a brand new presentation and he closed 80% of the people for one-on-one appointments. Before he met me, his plan was not getting off the ground and he felt like he was stuck at the London Heathrow airport. But now, because of my help he is rocking and rolling.

I love speaking and training. Recently I was invited to speak at the congressional conferences in Maryland. I spoke at Bowie State University, Frostburg University and Morgan State University for Congressman Steny Hoyer, Roscoe Bartlett and Elijah E. Cummings. At these events, I spoke for about an hour and each time I told my story of how I came with just $20 and not a word of English. I taught how to build a multi-million dollar business. They expected me to just speak and lecture instead I danced with them by choosing songs like The Wobble Indian style. I played Bollywood music and told my audience I love you. After these events everyone came up to me and said thank you for rocking my world.

I recently did a nine and a half hour Sell Like Crazy Academy Live, in Columbia, MD. We had 30 who made a commitment to invest in their education. I was confident if they made a commitment to come to my event, they can attend the entire event, have a great time, write on my workbook, and pay me at the end of the event. Now that's CRAZY but to top that off, I said to the people that if they came and did not walk away with added value in their life all they have to do is come up to me and just return the workbook AND I will pay their gas money back. But rest assured, we rocked the entire day. I built this academy to not only just speak and teach but to implement every single step on the spot. During the event these attendees did not wait until the end to pay but they paid at the first break. I rock their world because I love to do so. On that note, I would love to do the same for you when you come to my

Live event you can visit

www.FinancialChakras.com for more information.

I love to stimulate and excite the world of my financial clients. I primarily specialize in showing people how not to lose any money in any market condition. In the 2008 Crash my strategy came to the test and I lost ZERO dollars for my clients. My clients are concerned about protecting their hard earned assets, estate taxes, probate, making sure that they will not run out of money in their old age, having lifetime income, reducing taxes on matters like Social Security, and last but not least, leaving a legacy for their kids and grandkids.

In 2004, when I started my own firm, I did an event where 200 people showed up over a period of four events. From which I created my first clients, Mr. and Mrs. Lewis. They were in their 60's and their concern was to protect what they had and pass it on to their kids without going through probate. Well, we did just that. We not only did not lose money for them but grew their money from X to X+Y. From 2004 to now we have been growing their money and locking it in every single year. Not only that but when Mr. Lewis passed away all the money that he had put with me went directly to his beneficiaries without going to probate. Mrs. Lewis is still my client and continues to enjoy keeping her hard earned retirement dollars safe and secure. I am proud to say I rocked her world when she did not have to go through probate with her money. Instead all she had to do was fill out a form and we were done.

In 2008, I arranged a birthday party for a client of mine. This client had about 10 friends show up for her birthday. One of the friends after this party decided to meet with me. They told me they were concerned with their money in the market, making sure she can have lifetime income, and taxes on their Social Security income. I was able to show them how to not lose money in the market and eliminate her Social Security taxes completely. Now she has grown her money from X to X + Y. Now she can be sure that she will not run out of money in her old age. On top of that, I helped her eliminate taxes on Social Security.

Just recently, I was talking to a young boomer who is also a business owner and an existing client of mine. He has been with me since 2006. When we met, his needs were simple. He wanted to keep his money, and to not lose it. We accomplished that.

He needed to make sure that his estate taxes are taken care of because his assets are in the millions and now he is ready to plan for his changing situation. I am able to help him put vehicles in place that will not only give his kids more then what he planned, but also secure his retirement in a way that he will have more income than he ever. I love rocking his world and making a positive impact.

$80,000 per Year More

I have a young business owner who is my client. It took four years of follow-up before he became my financial services client. He wanted the same things as others, safety of money, unbelievable growth, not running out of money, and leaving a legacy for his kids. Well, I helped him get $80,000 per year more than his original plan in his retirement. He and his family are thankful for the work I have done for them. I rocked their world, too!

I can go on and on, but… this is what it is all about. I love to get you to that level where you are rocking and rolling in your world. I get jazzed up when I get to help you. There is nothing more thrilling than knowing that I can help you through my Sell Like Crazy

Academy or having you as a financial services client. Please keep in mind that the examples above are from real clients. However, each client's situation is different and I am sure yours is unique too. Therefore, the results will vary based on your circumstances. My commitment to you is be honest, open, and transparent.

Go out there with a bang! I know you can do it. If I came here with just $20 and not a word English and built my empire, then why can't you? Listen, go out there and align the chakras Heart, Head, and the Gut and you too can rock your client's world. Keep them in that order and you can accomplish anything that you want.

I want to thank you for taking the time to read this book. I want to give you a special invitation to come to my event Sell Like Crazy Academy. As a special thanks, all you have to do is just visit www. FinancialChakras.com and you will be able to register for this two-day exclusive event.

If you want help in your financial matters just visit my site www. FinancialChakras.com, submit a request for us to meet and I will be happy to schedule a meeting with you.

If you have any other questions and want to get in touch with me, just send e-mail to Ash@FinancialChakras.com.

I can't thank you enough for reading this book and passing the word along to your friends and family members.

As I wobble my way out of this book, my family and I want to thank you, once again, for reading this book.

Be sure to visit www.FinancialChakras.com and join us at the next Sell Like Crazy Academy. It's CRAZY!!!!!